Contents

4   Amazing Grace

6   Cripple Creek

8   Devil's Dream

10   Frankie and Johnny

12   Frosty Morning

14   Overall the Waterfall

16   Short'nin' Bread

18   Stone's Rag

20   MANDOLIN NOTATION LEGEND

Amazing Grace

Words by John Newton
Traditional American Melody

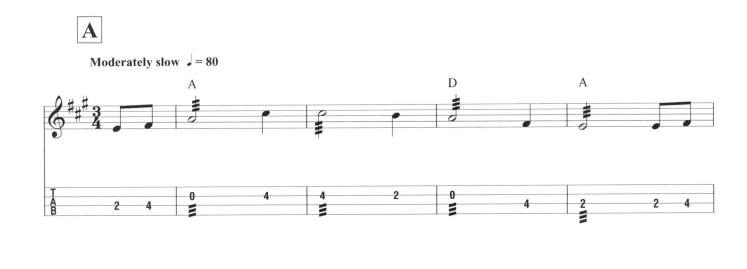

HAL•LEONARD®

MANDOLIN

PLAY-ALONG

AUDIO
ACCESS
INCLUDED

PLAYBACK+
Speed • Pitch • Balance • Loop

SONGS FOR
Beginners

VOL. 10

To access audio visit:
www.halleonard.com/mylibrary

Enter Code
4346-4664-3559-3983

Arranged and recorded by Guy Fiorentini

ISBN 978-1-4950-5944-5

HAL•LEONARD®

7777 W. BLUEMOUND RD. P.O. BOX 13819 MILWAUKEE, WI 53213

In Australia Contact:
Hal Leonard Australia Pty. Ltd.
4 Lentara Court
Cheltenham, Victoria, 3192 Australia
Email: ausadmin@halleonard.com.au

Visit Hal Leonard Online at
www.halleonard.com

Open Strings and Alternate Fingerings

The first three (pairs of) open strings give us notes that can also be played at the 7th fret of the previous string. For example, we find the same A at both the open 2nd string and the 7th fret of the third string. This gives us different options for playing the same melodic lines.

In Example 1 below (measures 9-12 from "Stones Rag") we find the A played in both places; Example 2 provides alternate fingerings.

Example 1

Example 2

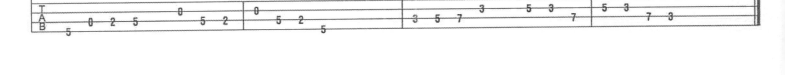

While playing an open string is easier in terms of fretting, it sometimes makes picking more difficult. Often this is a matter of playing on fewer strings, like in the first two measures above. Examples 3 and 4 (from "Frosty Morning") further illustrate this: although there is more left hand movement in example 3, it's easier to pick at moderate to higher tempos. Additionally, the consistent down-up-down picking makes for better tone.

Example 3

Example 4

B

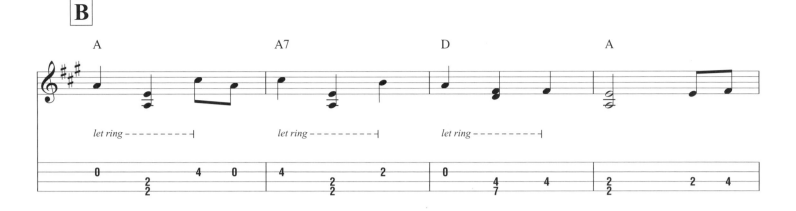

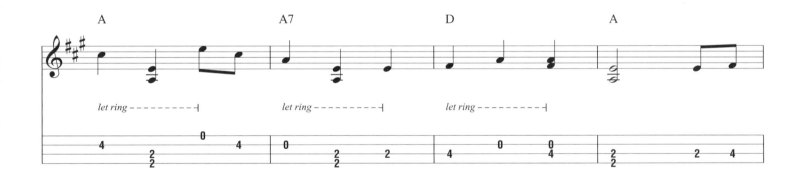

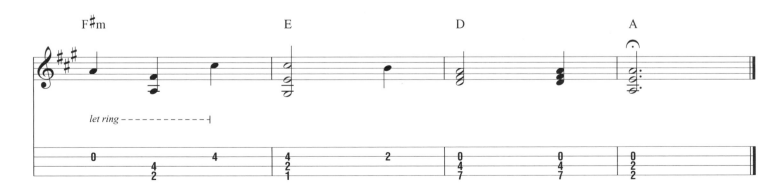

Cripple Creek

American Fiddle Tune

A

Moderately fast ♩ = 150

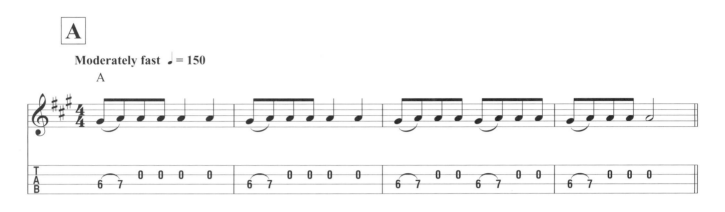

B

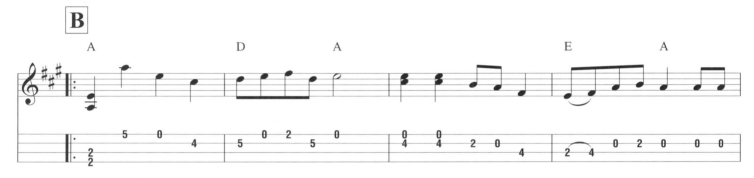

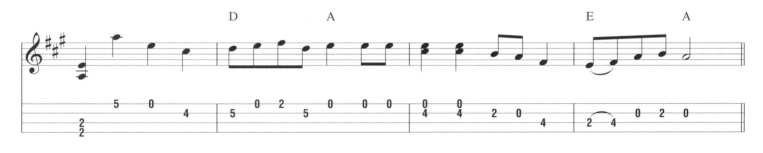

C

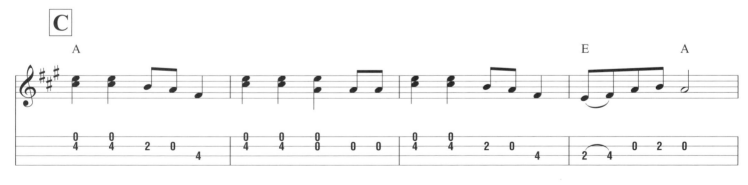

1.

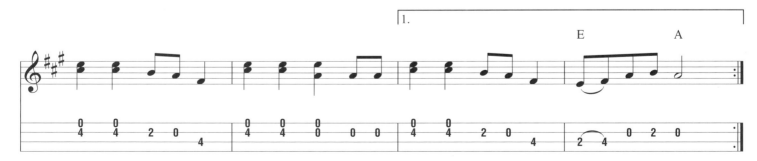

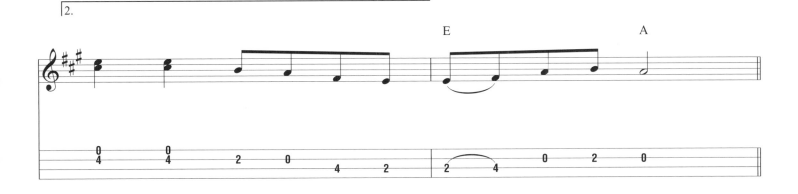

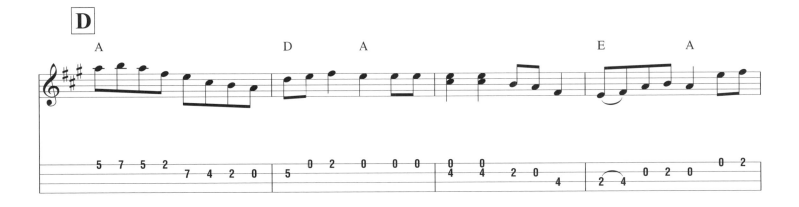

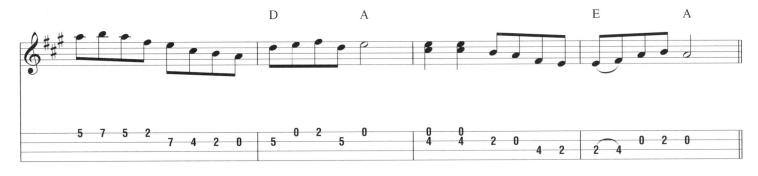

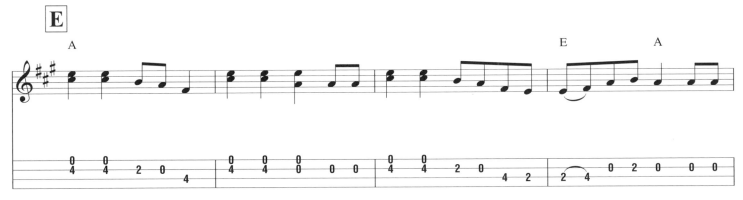

Devil's Dream

Traditional

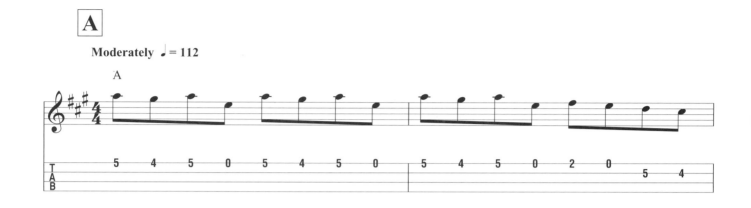

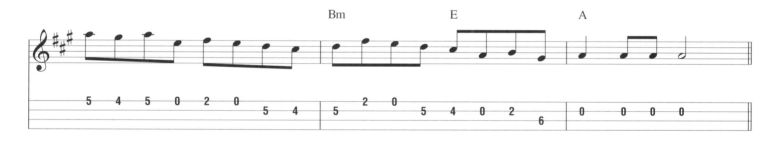

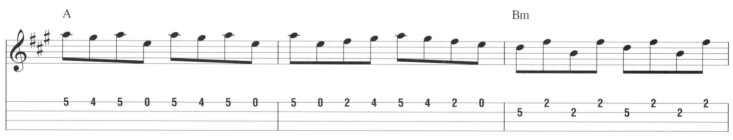

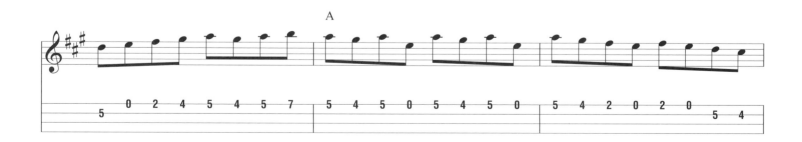

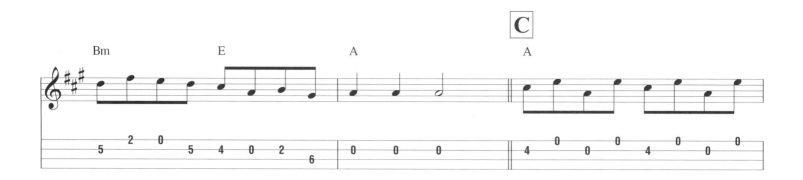

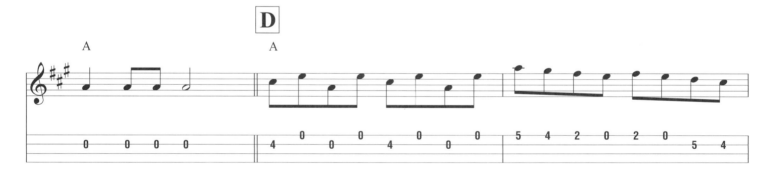

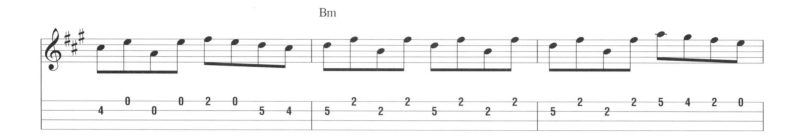

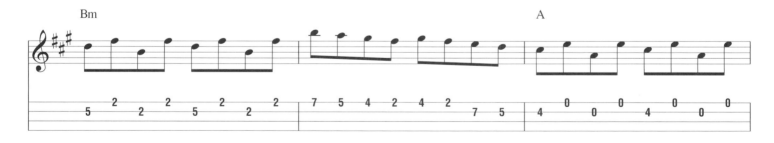

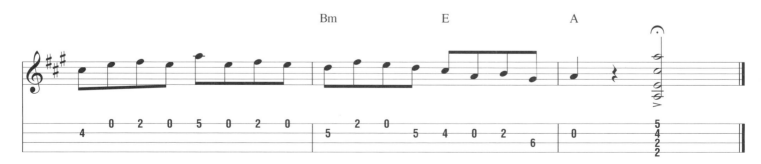

Frankie and Johnny

Anonymous Blues Ballad

B

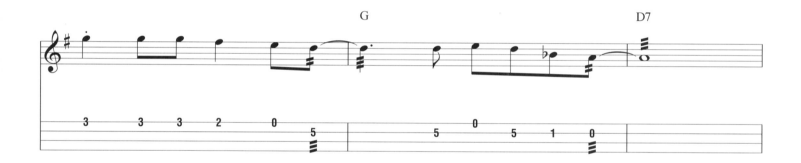

Frosty Morning

Traditional Fiddle Tune

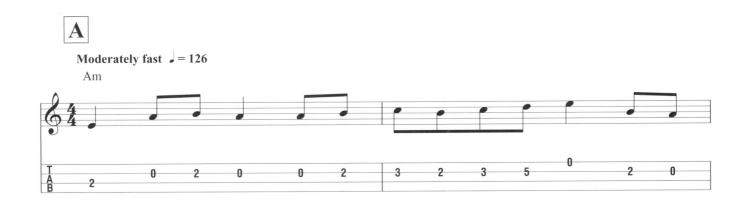

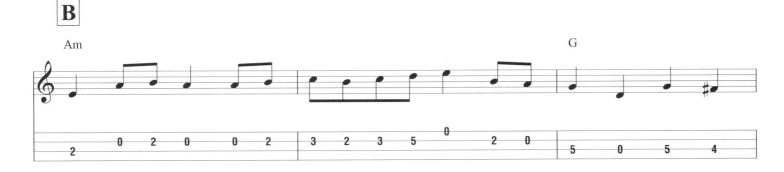

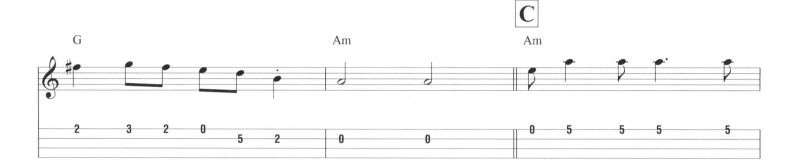

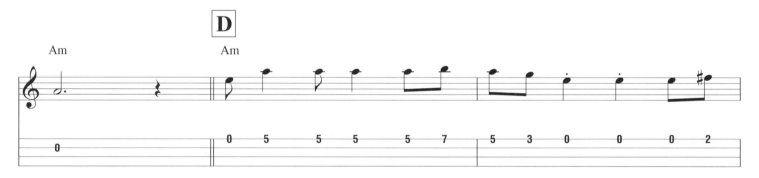

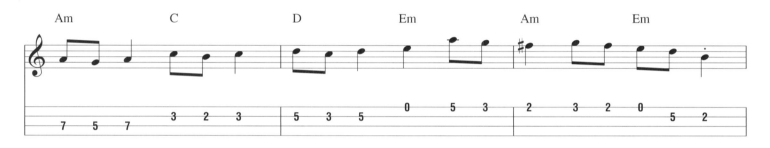

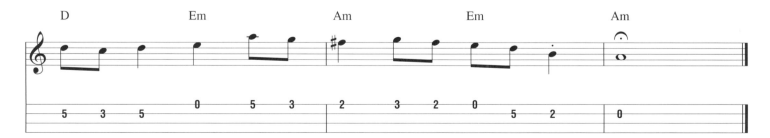

Over the Waterfall

Traditional Fiddle Tune

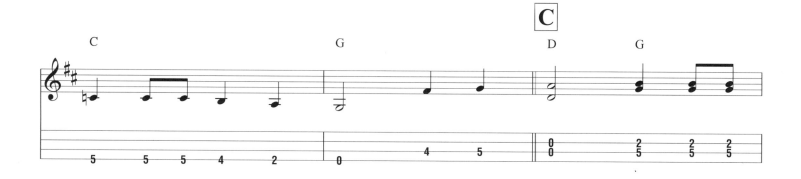

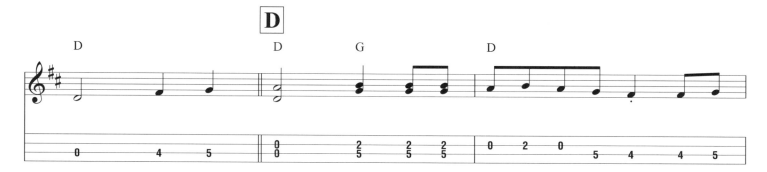

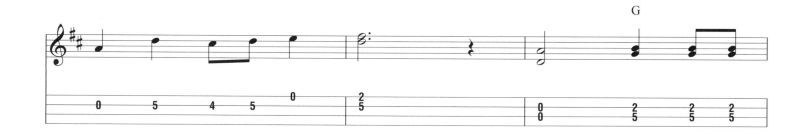

Short'nin' Bread

Plantation Song

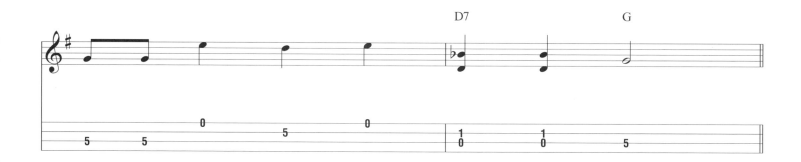

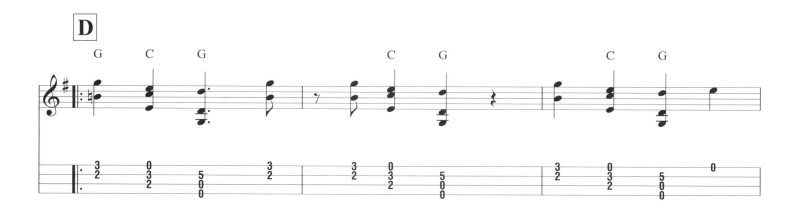

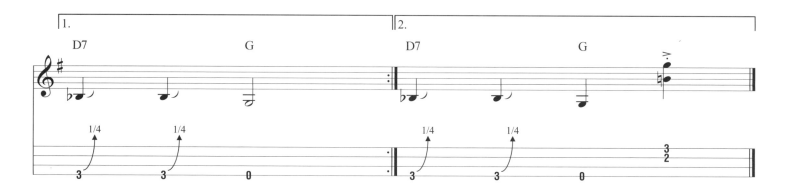

Stone's Rag

Traditional

*Measures 1-2 may be substituted here.

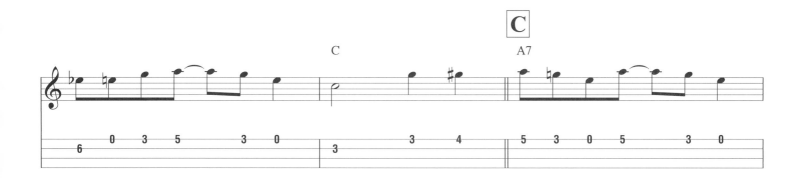

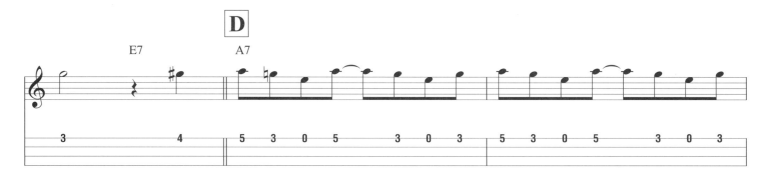

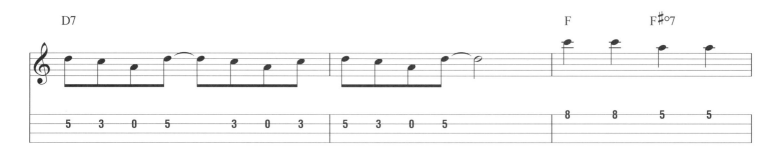

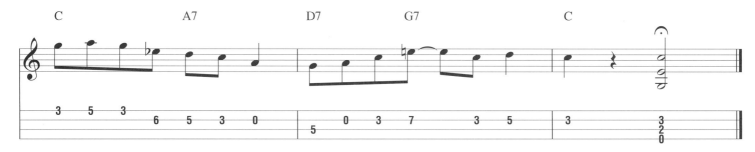

MANDOLIN NOTATION LEGEND

Mandolin music can be notated three different ways: on a *musical staff*, in *tablature*, and in *rhythm slashes*.

RHYTHM SLASHES are written above the staff. Strum chords in the rhythm indicated. Use the chord diagrams found at the top of the first page of the transcription for the appropriate chord voicings.

THE MUSICAL STAFF shows pitches and rhythms and is divided by bar lines into measures. Pitches are named after the first seven letters of the alphabet.

TABLATURE graphically represents the mandolin fretboard. Each of the four horizontal lines represents each of the four courses of strings, and each number represents a fret.

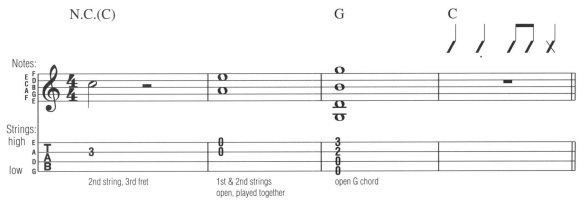

2nd string, 3rd fret   1st & 2nd strings open, played together   open G chord

Definitions for Special Mandolin Notation

MUTED STRING(S): Lightly touch a string with the edge of your fret-hand finger while fretting a note on an adjacent string, causing the muted string to be unheard. Muting all of the strings with the fingers of the fret-hand while strumming the strings with the picking hand produces a percussive effect.

HAMMER-ON: Strike the first (lower) note with one finger, then sound the higher note (on the same string) with another finger by fretting it without picking.

PULL-OFF: Place both fingers on the notes to be sounded. Strike the first note and, without picking, pull the finger off to sound the second (lower) note.

LEGATO SLIDE: Strike the first note and then slide the same fret-hand finger up or down to the second note. The second note is not struck.

SHIFT SLIDE: Same as the legato slide except the second note is struck.

HALF-STEP BEND: Strike the note and bend up ½ step.

GRACE NOTE BEND: Strike the note and immediately bend up as indicated.

TREMOLO PICKING: The note is picked rapidly and continuously.

Additional Musical Definitions

p (piano)	• Play quietly.
mp (mezzo-piano)	• Play moderately quiet.
mf (mezzo-forte)	• Play moderately loud.
f (forte)	• Play loudly.
cont. rhy. sim.	• Continue strumming in similar rhythm.
N.C. *(no chord)*	• Don't strum until the next chord symbol. Chord symbols in parentheses reflect implied harmony.
D.S. al Coda	• Go back to the sign (𝄋), then play until the measure marked *"To Coda"*, then skip to the section labeled **"Coda."**
D.S.S. al Coda 2	• Go back to the double sign (𝄋𝄋), then play until the measure marked *"To Coda 2"*, then skip to the section labeled **"Coda 2."**
D.S. al Fine	• Go back to the sign (𝄋), then play until the label *"Fine."*

(staccato) • Play the note or chord short.

rit.

(ritard) • Gradually slow down.

(fermata) • Hold the note or chord for an undetermined amount of time.

• Repeat measures between signs.

• When a repeated section has different endings, play the first ending only the first time and the second ending only the second time.

NOTE: Tablature numbers in parentheses mean:
1. The note is being sustained over a system (note in standard notation is tied), or
2. The note is sustained, but a new articulation (such as a hammer-on, pull-off or slide) begins.

Hal Leonard Mandolin Play-Along Series

The Mandolin Play-Along Series will help you play your favorite songs quickly and easily. Just follow the written music, listen to the CD or online audio to hear how the mandolin should sound, and then play along using the separate backing tracks. Standard notation and tablature are both included in the book. The audio is enhanced so users can adjust the recording to any tempo without changing the pitch!

INCLUDES TAB

1. BLUEGRASS

Angeline the Baker • Billy in the Low Ground • Blackberry Blossom • Fisher's Hornpipe • Old Joe Clark • Salt Creek • Soldier's Joy • Whiskey Before Breakfast.
00702517 Book/CD Pack....................$14.99

2. CELTIC

A Fig for a Kiss • The Kesh Jig • Morrison's Jig • The Red Haired Boy • Rights of Man • Star of Munster • The Star of the County Down • Temperence Reel.
00702518 Book/CD Pack....................$14.99

3. POP HITS

Brown Eyed Girl • I Shot the Sheriff • In My Life • Mrs. Robinson • Stand by Me • Superstition • Tears in Heaven • You Can't Hurry Love.
00702519 Book/CD Pack....................$14.99

4. J.S. BACH

Bourree in E Minor • Invention No.1 (Bach) • Invention No.2 (Bach) • Jesu, Joy of Man's Desiring • March in D Major • Minuet in G • Musette in D Major • Sleepers, Awake (Wachet Auf).
00702520 Book/CD Pack....................$14.99

5. GYPSY SWING

After You've Gone • Avalon • China Boy • Dark Eyes • Indiana (Back Home Again in Indiana) • Limehouse Blues • The Sheik of Araby • Tiger Rag (Hold That Tiger).
00702521 Book/CD Pack....................$14.99

6. ROCK HITS

Back in the High Life Again • Copperhead Road • Going to California • Ho Hey • Iris • Losing My Religion • Maggie May • Sunny Came Home.
00119367 Book/Online Audio $16.99

7. ITALIAN CLASSICS

Come Back to Sorrento • La Spagnola • Mattinata • 'O Sole Mio • Oh Marie • Santa Lucia • Tarantella • Vieni Sul Mar.
00119368 Book/CD Pack....................$16.99

8. MANDOLIN FAVORITES

Arrivederci Roma (Goodbye to Rome) • The Godfather (Love Theme) • Misirlou • Never on Sunday • Over the Rainbow • Spanish Eyes • That's Amoré (That's Love) • Theme from "Zorba the Greek."
00119494 Book/CD Pack....................$14.99

9. CHRISTMAS CAROLS

Angels We Have Heard on High • Carol of the Bells • Go, Tell It on the Mountain • Hark! the Herald Angels Sing • Joy to the World • O Holy Night • Silent Night • We Wish You a Merry Christmas.
00119895 Book/CD Pack....................$14.99

11. CLASSICAL THEMES

Blue Danube Waltz • Eine Kleine Nachtmusik ("Serenade"), First Movement Excerpt • Für Elise • Humoresque • In the Hall of the Mountain King • La donna e mobile • The Merry Widow Waltz • Spring, First Movement.
00156777 Book/Online Audio $14.99

HAL•LEONARD®
CORPORATION
7777 W. BLUEMOUND RD. P.O. BOX 13819
MILWAUKEE, WISCONSIN 53213

www.halleonard.com

101 TIPS FROM HAL LEONARD

STUFF ALL THE PROS KNOW AND USE

Ready to take your skills to the next level? These books present valuable how-to insight that musicians of all styles and levels can benefit from. The text, photos, music, diagrams and accompanying audio provide a terrific, easy-to-use resource for a variety of topics.

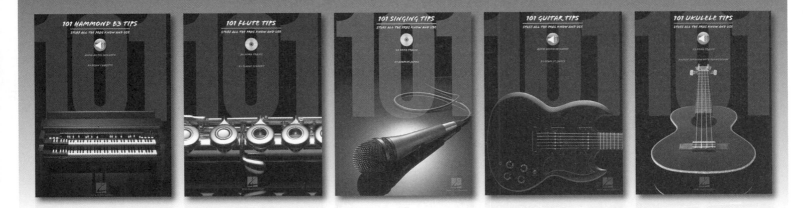

101 HAMMOND B-3 TIPS
by Brian Charette
Topics include: funky scales and modes; unconventional harmonies; creative chord voicings; cool drawbar settings; ear-grabbing special effects; professional gigging advice; practicing effectively; making good use of the pedals; and much more!
00128918 Book/Online Audio $14.99

101 HARMONICA TIPS
by Steve Cohen
Topics include: techniques, position playing, soloing, accompaniment, the blues, equipment, performance, maintenance, and much more!
00821040 Book/CD Pack..................................$16.99

101 CELLO TIPS—2ND EDITION
by Angela Schmidt
Topics include: bowing techniques, non-classical playing, electric cellos, accessories, gig tips, practicing, recording and much more!
00149094 Book/Online Audio $14.99

101 FLUTE TIPS
by Elaine Schmidt
Topics include: selecting the right flute for you, finding the right teacher, warm-up exercises, practicing effectively, taking good care of your flute, gigging advice, staying and playing healthy, and much more.
00119883 Book/CD Pack..................................$14.99

101 SAXOPHONE TIPS
by Eric Morones
Topics include: techniques; maintenance; equipment; practicing; recording; performance; and much more!
00311082 Book/CD Pack..................................$14.95

101 SINGING TIPS
by Adam St. James
Topics include: vocal exercises, breathing exercises, the singer's health, preparation, technique, understanding music, singing harmony, microphones, career advice, and much more!
00740308 Book/CD Pack..................................$14.95

101 TRUMPET TIPS
by Scott Barnard
Topics include: techniques, articulation, tone production, soloing, exercises, special effects, equipment, performance, maintenance and much more.
00312082 Book/CD Pack...................................$14.99

101 UPRIGHT BASS TIPS
by Andy McKee
Topics include: right- and left-hand technique, improvising and soloing, practicing, proper care of the instrument, ear training, performance, and much more.
00102009 Book/Online Audio $14.99

101 BASS TIPS
by Gary Willis
Topics include: techniques, improvising and soloing, equipment, practicing, ear training, performance, theory, and much more.
00695542 Book/Online Audio $16.95

101 DRUM TIPS—2ND EDITION
by Scott Schroedl
Topics include: grooves, practicing, warming up, tuning, gear, performance, and much more!
00151936 Book/Online Audio $14.99

101 FIVE-STRING BANJO TIPS
by Fred Sokolow
Topics include: techniques, ear training, performance, and much more!
00696647 Book/CD Pack..................................$14.99

101 GUITAR TIPS
by Adam St. James
Topics include: scales, music theory, truss rod adjustments, proper recording studio set-ups, and much more. The book also features snippets of advice from some of the most celebrated guitarists and producers in the music business.
00695737 Book/Online Audio $16.95

101 MANDOLIN TIPS
by Fred Sokolow
Topics include: playing tips, practicing tips, accessories, mandolin history and lore, practical music theory, and much more!
00119493 Book/Online Audio $14.99

101 RECORDING TIPS
by Adam St. James
This book contains recording tips, suggestions, and advice learned firsthand from legendary producers, engineers, and artists. These tricks of the trade will improve anyone's home or pro studio recordings.
00311035 Book/CD Pack.................................$14.95

101 UKULELE TIPS
by Fred Sokolow with Ronny Schiff
Topics include: techniques, improvising and soloing, equipment, practicing, ear training, performance, uke history and lore, and much more!
00696596 Book/Online Audio $14.99

101 VIOLIN TIPS
by Angela Schmidt
Topics include: bowing techniques, non-classical playing, electric violins, accessories, gig tips, practicing, recording, and much more!
00842672 Book/CD Pack.................................$14.99

Prices, contents and availability subject to change without notice.

Learn To Play Today
with folk music instruction from

HAL·LEONARD®

Hal Leonard Banjo Method – Second Edition
Authored by Mac Robertson, Robbie Clement & Will Schmid. This innovative method teaches 5-string, bluegrass style. The method consists of two instruction books and two cross-referenced supplement books that offer the beginner a carefully-paced and interest-keeping approach to the bluegrass style.

Method Book 1
00699500 Book $7.99
00695101 Book/CD Pack $16.99

Method Book 2
00699502...$7.99

Supplementary Songbooks
00699515 Easy Banjo Solos..............................$9.99
00699516 More Easy Banjo Solos $9.99

Hal Leonard Dulcimer Method – Second Edition
by Neal Hellman
A beginning method for the Appalachian dulcimer with a unique new approach to solo melody and chord playing. Includes tuning, modes and many beautiful folk songs all demonstrated on the audio accompaniment. Music and tablature.
00699289 Book $8.99
00697230 Book/CD Pack $16.99

The Hal Leonard Complete Harmonica Method – Chromatic Harmonica
by Bobby Joe Holman
The only harmonica method to present the chromatic harmonica in 14 scales and modes in all 12 keys!
00841286 Book/Online Audio..............................$12.99

The Hal Leonard Complete Harmonica Method – The Diatonic Harmonica
by Bobby Joe Holman
This terrific method book/CD pack specific to the diatonic harmonica covers all six positions! It contains more than 20 songs and musical examples.
00841285 Book/CD Pack $12.95

Hal Leonard Fiddle Method
by Chris Wagoner
The Hal Leonard Fiddle Method is the perfect introduction to playing folk, bluegrass and country styles on the violin. Many traditional tunes are included to illustrate a variety of techniques. The accompanying audio includes many tracks for demonstration and play-along. Covers: instrument selection and care; playing positions; theory; slides & slurs; shuffle feel; bowing; drones; playing "backup"; cross-tuning; and much more!
00311415 Book $5.99
00311416 Book/Online Audio..............................$9.99

The Hal Leonard Mandolin Method – Second Edition
Noted mandolinist and teacher Rich Del Grosso has authored this excellent mandolin method that features great playable tunes in several styles (bluegrass, country, folk, blues) in standard music notation and tablature. The audio features play-along duets.
00699296 Book $7.99
00695102 Book/Online Audio $15.99

Hal Leonard Oud Method
by John Bilezikjian
This book teaches the fundamentals of standard Western music notation in the context of oud playing. It also covers: types of ouds, tuning the oud, playing position, how to string the oud, scales, chords, arpeggios, tremolo technique, studies and exercises, songs and rhythms from Armenia and the Middle East, and a CD with 25 tracks for demonstration and play along.
00695836 Book/CD Pack $12.99

Hal Leonard Ukulele Method Book 1
by Lil' Rev
INCLUDES TAB
This comprehensive and easy-to-use beginner's guide by acclaimed performer and uke master Lil' Rev includes many fun songs of different styles to learn and play. Includes: types of ukuleles, tuning, music reading, melody playing, chords, strumming, scales, tremolo, music notation and tablature, a variety of music styles, ukulele history and much more.
00695847 Book $6.99
00695832 Book/Online Audio..............................$10.99

HAL·LEONARD®
CORPORATION
7777 W. BLUEMOUND RD. P.O. BOX 13819 MILWAUKEE, WI 53213

Visit Hal Leonard Online at
www.halleonard.com

Prices and availability subject to change without notice.